HOW
TO DRAW
A GRAPHIC
NOVEL

First published in the United States of America in 2023 by
Thames & Hudson Inc., 500 Fifth Avenue, New York, New York 10110

How to Draw a Graphic Novel © 2023 BesideBooks S.r.l, Italy
Text by Balthazar Pagani © 2023 BesideBooks S.r.l, Italy
Design by Bebung © 2023 BesideBooks S.r.l, Italy
Text and illustrations by Otto Gabos © 2023 Otto Gabos
Illustrations by Marco Maraggi © 2023 Marco Maraggi

Interview and illustrations by Nina Bunjevac © 2023 Nina Bunjevac
Interview and illustrations by Peter Kuper © 2023 Peter Kuper
Interview and illustrations by Elisa Macellari © 2023 Elisa Macellari
Interview and illustrations by Ben Passmore © 2023 Ben Passmore
Interview and illustrations by Kan Takahama © 2023 Kan Takahama

Translated by Howard Curtis
Ken Takahama interview translated from the Japanese by Helena Simmonds
The author would like to thank Marco Ficarra for his valuable suggestions
and technical information

Library of Congress Control Number 2023935421

ISBN 978-0-500-66020-1

Printed and bound in China by Toppan Leefung Printing Limited

Be the first to know about our new releases,
exclusive content and author events by visiting
thamesandhudson.com
thamesandhudsonusa.com
thamesandhudson.com.au

ILLUSTRATIONS BY
MARCO MARAGGI

HOW TO DRAW A GRAPHIC NOVEL

BALTHAZAR PAGANI

WITH PRO TIPS BY
OTTO GABOS

CONTENTS

INTRODUCTION

WHAT IS A GRAPHIC NOVEL?

There are many ways of telling a story: through novels, films, plays, podcasts...
One other way is through graphic novels.

Both a genre and a narrative technique, **the graphic novel is a self-contained story told in comics**. This means that the story is of fundamental importance. It has the narrative plot typical of a novel and it is told through the visual language of comics.

American cartoonist Will Eisner once called comics "sequential art," while Scott McCloud dedicated his beautiful and essential book *Understanding Comics* to understanding and explaining the nature of this wonderful art form. I think every author has their own vision and definition of what a graphic novel is. I imagine you will have your own, too.

Producing graphic novels is also an attitude. The aim of this book is to give you a few pointers on how to realize your own inclinations, to arouse your curiosity, and deepen your knowledge of graphic novels. I also want to provide you with a few basic tools so that you can develop a story, combine texts and drawings, and end up with your own graphic novel.

Don't be shy, and don't be modest: you can create a graphic novel too, this is just the beginning. From small acorns, large oaks grow!

Balthazar Pagani

A QUICK HISTORY OF COMICS

When we say **GRAPHIC NOVELS ARE A WORLD IN AND OF THEMSELVES,** we're not wrong. There are well-trodden places in this world and much less-known ones; some have a long history behind them and others have a great future ahead of them. And then there are the great protagonists of this world: the readers who discovered it, and the authors and artists who are building it. **LET OUR EXPLORATION OF GRAPHIC NOVELS BEGIN!**

GENRES, STORIES AND THEMES

No genre is off limits for a graphic novel. From the most classic to the most experimental; from those that are for a wide audience to those that are more niche. A genre is defined by its themes, its subjects, its characters, and its target audience.

Some of us are omnivores and sample everything, while others find their favorite genre and never abandon it. But be careful: in the world of graphic novels, you might get hooked! Luckily for us, comic books aren't as bad for us as sugary drinks, so we can try as many different genres as we like!

COMIC
SMOOTHIES

ADVENTURE
CRIME
NOIR
HUMOR
SCIENCE FICTION
SUPERHEROES
FANTASY
DYSTOPIAS
CYBERPUNK
HORROR
ROMANCE
WESTERN
INDIE/ALTERNATIVE

Genres reflect the tastes of those who write and those who read graphic novels. The following list isn't official, but understanding the different genres will definitely help you find what you're looking for in a bookstore or library. So they're useful as an indication, but you should use your own judgment too.

THE GREAT GRAPHIC NOVEL NATIONS

EVERY COUNTRY HAS ITS OWN STYLE OF COMICS... Up until a few decades ago this was a well-established truth. Today, as in many other fields, old borders are disappearing but it's always good to remind ourselves of where the journey started.

UNITED STATES OF AMERICA

In the United States the success of comics is closely linked to the birth—and the success!—of **superheroes**. In the 1930s, during what is known as the "golden age of comics," Superman, Batman and Wonder Woman start to appear in DC Comics and All-American Comics.

In the 1950s the company that will later become Marvel starts to publish comics. This period sees the arrival of Spiderman, Iron Man, Captain America, Hulk, the X-Men, and the Fantastic Four, among others. The world will never be the same again!

JAPAN

In Japan, comics go by the name of **manga**. The term "manga" dates back to the 18th century, and was most famously used by 19th century artist **Hokusai** to describe his illustrated books. However, we have to wait until the 1950s for manga to become really popular. Today there are hundreds of sub-genres of manga and they all share certain distinct characteristics.

Manga stories are published in episodes. They are generally drawn in black and white, and the characters often have large eyes and childlike features, even though manga is intended for an adult audience. Manga also reads right to left, the opposite direction from Western texts. Some manga series have given rise to animated versions, hence the name "**anime**," which is an abbreviation of *animēshon*, a Japanese transliteration of *animation*.

EUROPE

Rodolphe Töpffer is considered to be the first graphic novel author in Europe, with his book *Les Amours de Monsieur Vieux Bois*, published in 1827. Since then, the genre has developed in a thousand different directions. What ties them together is that there is no single paradigm of what a graphic novel should be. **In Europe the success of the graphic novel depends entirely on the author.**

ARE YOU READY TO BECOME THE NEXT GREAT GRAPHIC NOVELIST? DON'T WASTE ANY TIME! GO STRAIGHT TO A BOOKSTORE OR LIBRARY AND SEARCH FOR GRAPHIC NOVELS.

BEFORE YOU START DRAWING

Creative inspiration doesn't follow predefined rules or regular work hours, but producing a graphic novel ISN'T PURELY A CREATIVE MATTER. It involves good working methods, too. Before you start drawing you will need to research your subject matter and work on the writing and drawing styles in order to create HARMONY BETWEEN THE TWO ELEMENTS. You'll also need to understand some technical details about how to set up your files.

ARTIST OR WRITER: WHICH ONE ARE YOU?

We all have a range of talents. The question is, what are your strengths? For example... **are you good at drawing?** Or did you learn just enough in elementary school to draw a heart on a birthday card for your mother?

How are you with words? Do you describe emotions that you've never felt before, just for the fun of it, or does a blank page send you into a panic?

THE ILLUSTRATOR

Drawing, like writing, is a talent, and every talent we have needs to be nurtured (that's why you have this book, isn't it?). Not many people are good at both drawing and writing, although with practice and enthusiasm we can learn to do anything.

If you can draw and don't like writing, you are an **artist**, pure and simple. If you want to create a graphic novel, you will need to find a writer to work with you—in other words, someone who can write the text for the balloons and the panels, and someone who can give you clear directions for the storyboard, the framing of each scene, and the sequence of images.

THE AUTHOR

If you can write and don't like drawing, **your talent might be as a writer**. You will still need to find an artist to collaborate with—someone who can give shape to your text, interpret it, and make the characters unique.

THE COLLABORATION

The writer and the artist need to work together in harmony, influencing each other. It helps if they like each other, or else there will be trouble! But there's also a third option—if you enjoy both drawing and writing you may want to create a graphic novel entirely by yourself. So much the better, because you won't have to argue with anyone over a page . . . just make sure your publishers pay you twice the price!

A book, any book, is a magical object. It has the power to transport you to parallel universes, experience life in different time periods, and meet people you never would have imagined encountering.

A graphic novel can do even more. It can make you see things that don't exist, or that can't exist. Drawing can give form to people and places, to states of mind, and to sensations that can only be imagined.

DO YOU SEE WHAT I SEE?

... I THINK SO!

So it doesn't matter whether the idea for your graphic novel is realistic or not. What matters is that you can realize it through the combination of words and images.

Once you've settled on the idea for your graphic novel, the next step is to begin work on the **storyline**. The storyline is a short description (no more than a page of text) of the whole story, without any dialogue. It should outline the basic elements of the story: state where and when it is set, introduce the main characters, and explain what the protagonist's mission is.

After working out the storyline, you can move on to the **research** phase. This involves collecting **documentation**, so that you can write a believable text and draw characters and settings in an accurate way. If you want your graphic novel to be convincing, don't leave anything to chance.

SUBJECT, DOCUMENTATION, AND SCREENPLAY

Once the research phase is complete, you can begin writing the **script**. Script-writing conventions are well-defined. The script outlines not only the contents of the story but also instructions for how it should be told.

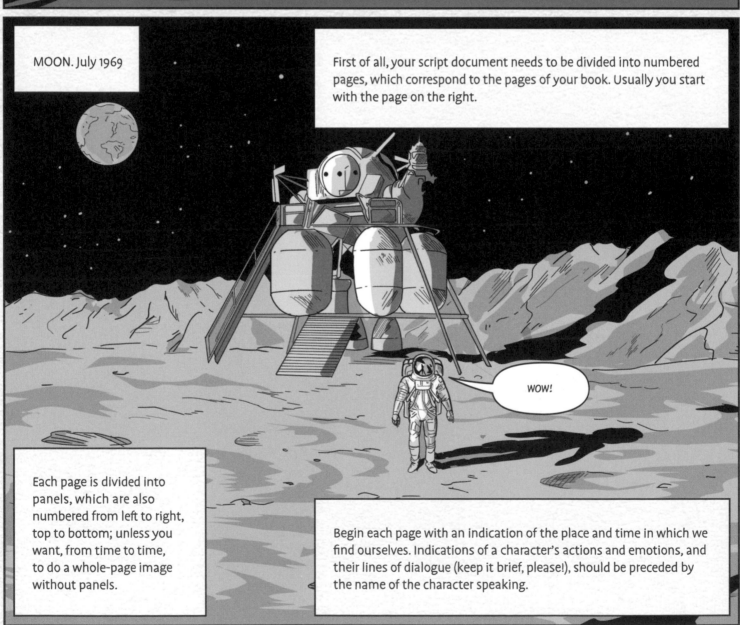

MOON. July 1969

First of all, your script document needs to be divided into numbered pages, which correspond to the pages of your book. Usually you start with the page on the right.

WOW!

Each page is divided into panels, which are also numbered from left to right, top to bottom; unless you want, from time to time, to do a whole-page image without panels.

Begin each page with an indication of the place and time in which we find ourselves. Indications of a character's actions and emotions, and their lines of dialogue (keep it brief, please!), should be preceded by the name of the character speaking.

Then we specify the **framing** of an illustration using initials that stand for:

DT: detail

MS: medium shot

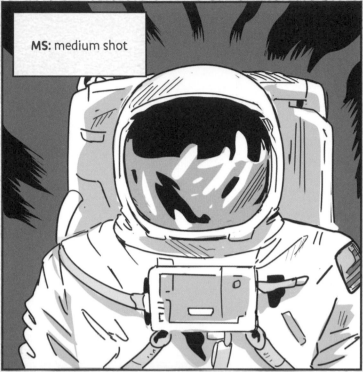

WF: whole figure

WS: wide shot

Before starting to draw, you may want to sketch out a **storyboard**. A storyboard doesn't need to be neat: it is a very rough preview of what the pages will eventually look like.

THE BASICS OF COPYRIGHT

Losing yourself in writing and drawing can give you a wonderful sense of power—you can create and destroy to your heart's content! The stories you're giving life to, and the actions of your characters, depend entirely on you. Cool, isn't it?

I'LL LOVE YOU FOREVER!

This phase can be really exciting, but be careful not to go too far . . .

HEY, YOU'VE DRAWN ME REALLY WELL. YOU'RE THE BEST ARTIST IN THE WORLD. YOU'RE DESTINED TO BECOME A MILLIONAIRE!

Above all, be very careful never to copy anything that has been created by someone else. This can happen without realizing it—you might feel inspired by an idea and forget where you first saw it. But imagine if another artist copied your work—you'd accuse them of plagiarism! If you want to include a quote, music lyrics, an artwork, or an illustration by another creator in your own work, you need to request permission from them first.

I'M SORRY, THE BOSS SAYS YOU CAN'T DO A COMIC BOOK VERSION OF GAME OF THRONES.

CLICK

THE BASICS OF PRINTING AND BINDING TECHNIQUES

A graphic novel can be published in print or online. Even if you intend to publish your story digitally, I would still advise you to work to the standards of paper printing, because if one day you decide to give your work a physical form, you won't have to go back over it.

The **pages** of a graphic novel are printed onto sheets of paper that are printed front and back, or "**double-sided**" printing as it's known in publishing.

The **cover** is normally printed **one-sided**. The artwork is a single file, composed of:
- **front cover**: features the title, the names of the author and illustrator, and the publisher's logo;
- **spine**: features the same text as the front cover; and
- **back cover**: containing the synopsis or "cover blurb," the barcode, and the price.

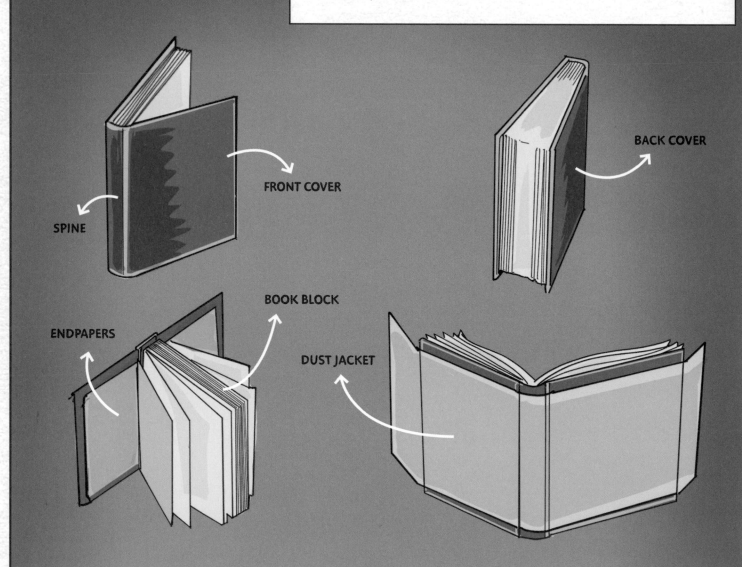

FRONT COVER

BACK COVER

SPINE

BOOK BLOCK

ENDPAPERS

DUST JACKET

A **hardback** book has a hard cover. The printed cover is glued to rough boards that form the front cover, back cover, and spine. It may also have a **dust jacket** that fits loosely over the top. **Endpapers** are glued to the cover boards and join the cover to the **book block**.

A **paperback** is a book with a soft cover—with or without **flaps**. There is no need for endpapers on a paperback book because the cover is glued directly to the inside pages.

What we normally call "color printing" is known in publishing as the **four-color process** because printing on paper uses four basic colors: cyan (C), magenta (M), yellow (Y) and key (black) (K), or **CMYK**. It's also possible to print special colors like fluorescents in addition to CMYK. As an alternative to the four-color process, a single color may be used (the classic black and white, for example), or else a two-color or three-color process, choosing combinations of the colors we like most.

The pages of a book are printed on large sheets. Each printed sheet is folded and cut along three of the four sides, to form a **section** of 16 pages. The section is sewn together with thread along the fourth side. Then all the sections that comprise a book are glued together along the sewed edges, forming the book block. The glue also attaches the book block to the cover. Alternatively, single sheets of paper can also be bound together, like in a notepad. But books bound this way tend to break easily and the pages can come loose.

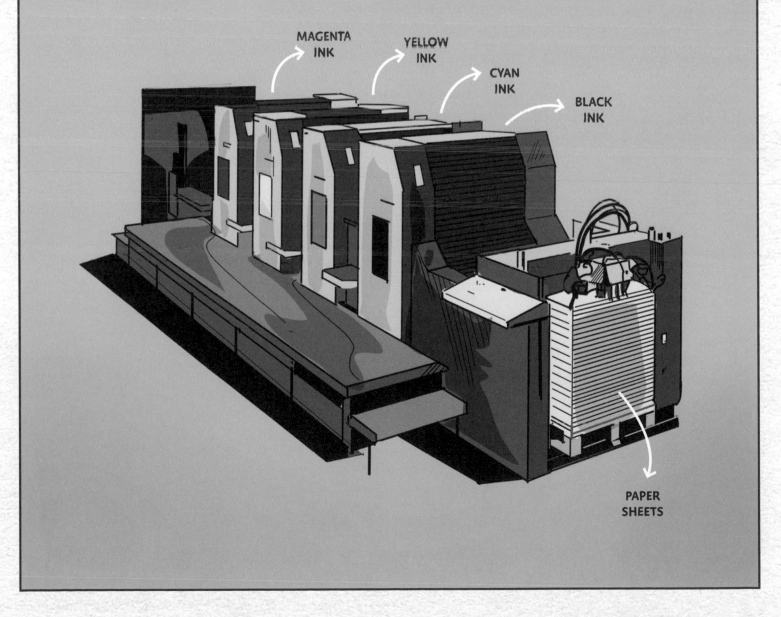

MAGENTA INK

YELLOW INK

CYAN INK

BLACK INK

PAPER SHEETS

Whether your original drawings are analog or digital, you will need to save them in a digital format before they can be placed in layout (see page 32). So it's important to know before you start how to save files in the correct way. When you plan your graphic novel, it is best to decide in advance what **format**, **page size**, and **page extent** (how many pages long) your book will be because these will all influence how you create your digital artwork files.

Drawings on paper need to be scanned digitally at a **high resolution**. Resolution is described in units of **DPI** or "dots per inch:"

- Color panels: 450 DPI
- Black and white panels: 1,200 DPI
- Grayscale* panels: 600 DPI

*grayscale describes a black-and-white image with gradients of tone

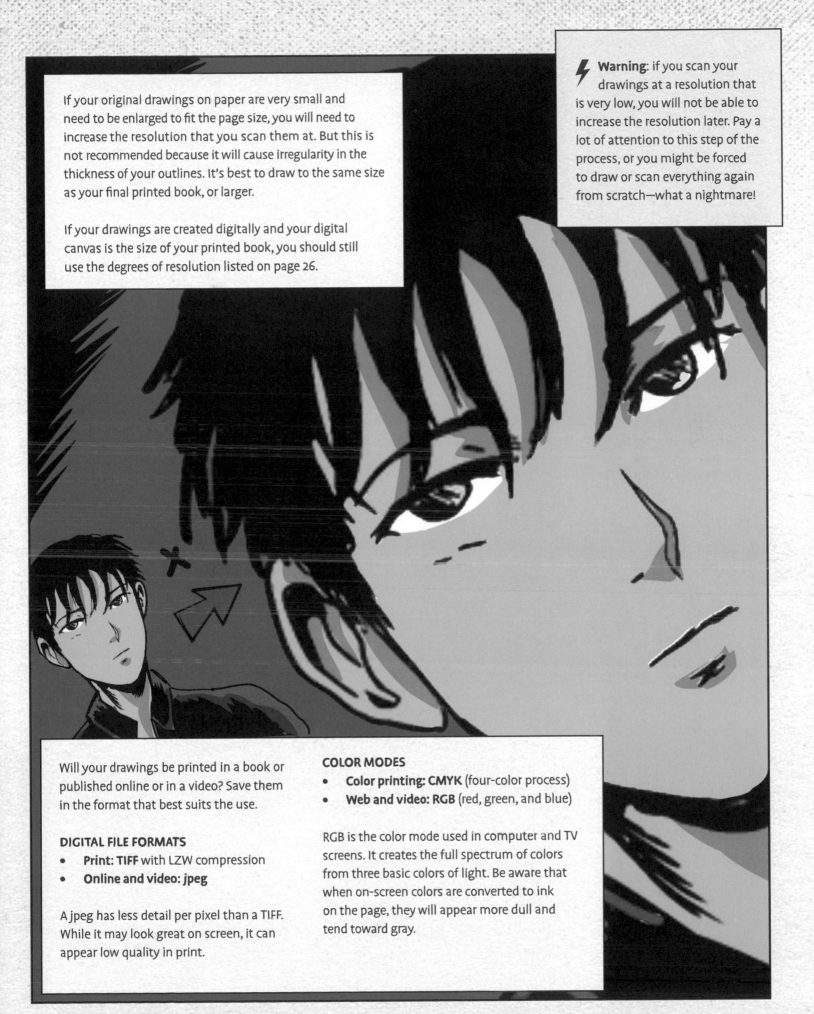

If your original drawings on paper are very small and need to be enlarged to fit the page size, you will need to increase the resolution that you scan them at. But this is not recommended because it will cause irregularity in the thickness of your outlines. It's best to draw to the same size as your final printed book, or larger.

If your drawings are created digitally and your digital canvas is the size of your printed book, you should still use the degrees of resolution listed on page 26.

⚡ **Warning**: if you scan your drawings at a resolution that is very low, you will not be able to increase the resolution later. Pay a lot of attention to this step of the process, or you might be forced to draw or scan everything again from scratch—what a nightmare!

Will your drawings be printed in a book or published online or in a video? Save them in the format that best suits the use.

DIGITAL FILE FORMATS
- **Print: TIFF** with LZW compression
- **Online and video: jpeg**

A jpeg has less detail per pixel than a TIFF. While it may look great on screen, it can appear low quality in print.

COLOR MODES
- **Color printing: CMYK** (four-color process)
- **Web and video: RGB** (red, green, and blue)

RGB is the color mode used in computer and TV screens. It creates the full spectrum of colors from three basic colors of light. Be aware that when on-screen colors are converted to ink on the page, they will appear more dull and tend toward gray.

THE BASICS OF WORKING

Creating a graphic novel involves **COMBINING TEXT AND IMAGE** within a page layout, in a format that is suitable to create a final file for printing. It takes a lot of care, attention, and precision. Before you start work on the final artwork for your graphic novel, there are **SOME BASIC THINGS YOU NEED TO KNOW** about page layout styles and typography that will influence how you work.

LAYOUT STYLES - PAGE FORMATS

PAGE FORMATS ARE
DESCRIBED AS 'PORTRAIT'
OR 'LANDSCAPE.'

Portrait
A rectangle that
is taller than it
is wide: classic
comic books.

Landscape
A rectangle that is wider than
it is tall: comic strip album.

Pages can also be square,
but most graphic novels
are portrait format.

COMMON
PAGE FORMATS

American: 6¾ in. (W) x 9½ in. (H)

French: 9½ in. (W) x 12⅝ in. (H)

Japanese: 4¾ in. (W) x 7⅛ in. (H)
or the larger 5¾ in. (W) x 8⅜ in. (H)

These page formats are distinguished not only by their size but also how the panels are **subdivided on the page**.

In **American superhero comic books**, the panels are usually laid out in **three horizontal strips** of varying sizes, and there are between **six and nine panels** per page.

In **French graphic novels**, the panels are laid out in **four strips**, and there are usually **eight or twelve panels** per page.

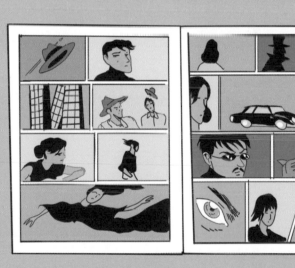

In **Japanese manga**, the page is smaller and pocket-sized. The pages are subdivided into **two or three strips** of panels and there are **between three and six panels** per page.

LAYOUT STYLES - PANELS

Each page in a graphic novel is composed of illustrations and text, arranged within **panels**. The size and number of panels on a page determine the **pace** of the narrative. Even the blank space between the panels can influence the speed and rhythm of your story.

Pace in a graphic novel depends on the speed at which we read the text and decipher the drawings. For example, if what's being shown is a dynamic fight scene, it's important not to use too many words, which would slow the action down.

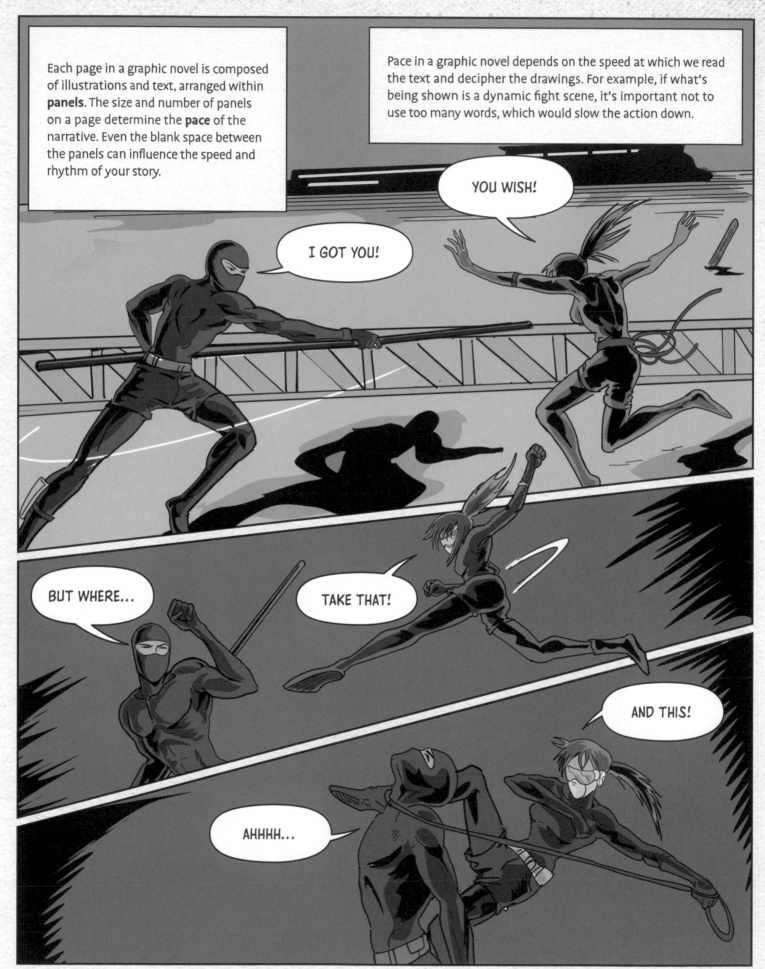

When you draw characters inside a panel, you need to take into account how much space is needed for the **balloons** that contain their dialogue.

WHERE ARE MY CAR KEYS?

UMMM...

COME ON!!!

DON'T RUSH ME...

And now where are we going to put the balloons?!?

Sometimes, to create a different rhythm, you might want to draw the panel without a border.

OH NO! SHE'S GONE NOW, AND I DON'T KNOW WHERE MY KEYS ARE!

LAYOUT STYLES - BALLOONS

The balloon contains the dialogue in a graphic novel. The reader's eye moves from one balloon to another, and thanks to the **tails** on the balloon, the reader knows who's speaking.

1

2

3

The graphic style of the balloon helps to give meaning to the words it contains.

I HAVE A NEW SONG.

The balloon of a normal dialogue is round.

If the balloon has a dotted line around it, then whoever's speaking is whispering.

OMG

If the voice is coming from a television or a computer, the border is usually drawn with lots of little spikes.

A cloud-shaped balloon means the character is thinking.

CREATE YOUR OWN FONT

Normally graphic novels are written in handmade fonts that feature only capital letters. To create a personalized font, you need to draw lots of faint parallel lines on a sheet of white cardboard and work with a black ink pen or a fine marker with a round tip.

Start drawing all the letters of the alphabet in capitals. Stay inside the lines—this will help you to draw each letter at a consistent size. Try a page full of As, then a page full of Bs... and so on. Fill whole pages until you establish a style of lettering that you're happy with.

Then go on to the numbers, accented letters, and the various symbols that make up a computer keyboard. Try to draw them in a regular, legible way.

Once you've finished doing this work, select the best examples of each letter, looking for the ones that are the most similar in style and thickness.

You can download simple software online that will generate a digital font from your hand-drawn letters. Although the process of creating your own font may take a while, it's worth it! Think of the time you will save in future.

GET STARTED

Now that you've learned the basics, the time has come for you to meet a **PROFESSIONAL GRAPHIC NOVELIST—OTTO GABOS.** Otto teaches comics in one of the oldest and most prestigious art schools in Europe and has written and drawn this chapter. With him, we'll discover the **ESSENTIAL TOOLS** for becoming a graphic novel artist, plus **SOME TOP TRICKS** of the trade before moving on to do some drawing exercises.

TRADITIONALLY, AND FOR PRACTICAL REASONS, MOST COMICS ARE DRAWN FIRST IN PENCIL AND ARE THEN GONE OVER IN BLACK INK. ORIGINALLY, THIS WAS BECAUSE A CLEAR MARK WITH STRONG CONTRAST WAS EASIER TO PRINT THAN A LIGHT MARK.

WHAT STARTED AS A TECHNICAL NECESSITY BECAME AN EXPRESSIVE AND STYLISTIC CHARACTERISTIC OF COMICS.

OBVIOUSLY, COMICS CAN BE DRAWN WITH ANY KIND OF GRAPHIC INSTRUMENT. DIGITAL IMAGES WILL BE DEALT WITH SEPARATELY.

Oils mixed with water

Gouache

Acrylics

Watercolors

Pastels

THE PHASES OF DRAWING:

First, the drawing is sketched in pencil.

Then the lines are gone over in black ink.

Finally, the pencil marks are rubbed out with an eraser. The paper you draw on is equally important. Paper can have a smooth, rough, or coated surface.

Micro pencil (the most common lead size is the 0,5)

Mechanical or propeling pencil

Regular pencil

Soft pencil (often 6B)

Your choice of pencil is crucial and is based on the hardness of the lead.

The thickness of the paper also varies from 40 lbs to 183 lbs.

For the phase of going over the drawing, or "inking," there are a vast range of instruments:

NIBS

Varied nibs

Nib holders

FELT TIP PENS

Markers

Fineliners

Gel pens

Nylon pens

Ballpoint pens

Fineliner tips

BRUSHES AND BRUSH PENS

Sable brushes (00, 0, 1, 2)

Dual-tip brush pens

Fude pens (used in Japanese calligraphy)

Pocket brush pens

Calligraphy brushes

A GOOD DRAWING BOARD WILL GIVE YOU A SMOOTH AND STURDY SURFACE TO DRAW ON. TO MAKE THE PROPORTIONS OF YOUR FIGURES MORE ACCURATE, IT'S BEST TO USE THE BOARD AT AN ANGLE.

NIB PENS AND BRUSHES NEED TO BE DIPPED IN INK. THERE ARE VARIOUS KINDS OF INK, THE MOST USEFUL ARE THE PERMANENT ONES. REMEMBER TO CLEAN ANY INSTRUMENTS WITH A CLOTH AFTER INKING—THIS WILL KEEP THEM WORKING SMOOTHLY.

TO MAKE PERFECTLY STRAIGHT LINES A RULER AND SET SQUARES ARE INDISPENSABLE!

Ink eraser

Kneaded eraser for details

Pencil eraser

DEVICES

A graphics tablet

A graphics tablet with a screen

An ordinary tablet, like an iPad

There are a variety of different devices you can use to draw digitally, ranging from basic models for amateurs to more sophisticated ones for professionals. Practically speaking, these tablets are your sheet of paper.

STYLUS PENS

A stylus pen is your digital pencil, pen, and brush. Look for a stylus with accurate pressure sensitivity—for example, the harder you press, the darker or thicker the line should appear. It's also important that there is little or no lag between your hand movement and the marks you make.

PROGRAMS

There are many programs and apps created especially for drawing graphic novels. They feature digital "brushes" that replicate different techniques, from watercolor and acrylic to pastels. There are also tools for drawing in perspective and creating lettering.

FANTASTIC, ISN'T IT? OF COURSE, BUT DON'T PRESUME YOU'LL BE ABLE TO DRAW COMPLICATED PANELS IN A MATTER OF MINUTES!

EVEN IF YOU USE DIGITAL TECHNIQUES, YOU STILL NEED TO STUDY, LEARN, AND EXPERIMENT, AND OF COURSE, MAKE MISTAKES. THAT'S THE BEST WAY TO HAVE FUN WHILE LEARNING.

ONCE UPON A TIME, WHEN ARTISTS HAD FINISHED DRAWING THE STORY, THEY WOULD SEND THEIR ILLUSTRATIONS TO THE PUBLISHER, WHO WOULD HANDLE ALL THE REST. NOW ARTISTS ARE MORE CLOSELY INVOLVED WITH THE FINISHED PRODUCT, AND THE DIGITAL POST-PRODUCTION STAGE HAS BECOME NOT ONLY AN UNAVOIDABLE NECESSITY BUT ALSO A GREAT CREATIVE OPPORTUNITY.

BY ADDING A FEW DIGITAL EFFECTS TO YOUR ANALOG DRAWINGS, YOU CAN ACHIEVE RESULTS THAT COMPLEMENT AND ENHANCE THE ORIGINAL GRAPHICS!

Analog

Analog + digital

First, draw everything on paper, imagining the potential interactions as you go.

Color washes can be added, details can be accentuated, and marks can be modified to increase the expressive range without distorting the original drawing.

You can use various analog techniques, as well as different media.

Colored pencil

Watercolor

Lead and charcoal

Scan your analog images in high definition and work on them digitally, cleaning them up, touching up the details, or even making major changes until you achieve your desired result.

The purpose of this mixed technique is to obtain the best from both traditional analog tools and digital ones, and to create something original that can easily be prepared for printing. The ultimate goal is to achieve the perfect blend—where it's difficult to distinguish what was drawn in analog from what was applied digitally. When you get it right, it's a real marvel!

Pastels and spot colors

India ink and spot colors

India ink and mezzotint

Lead pencil and watercolor

IN FACT, BY FUSING THE TWO APPROACHES, YOU WILL FIND AN INFINITE VARIETY OF STYLISTIC SOLUTIONS AVAILABLE TO YOU, CREATING A LASTING CONNECTION BETWEEN TRADITION AND INNOVATION.

✸ CHARACTER DESIGN

THERE ARE NO STORIES WITHOUT CHARACTERS. THEY MAY BE REAL OR IMAGINARY. THE IMPORTANT THING IS THAT THEY PERFORM ACTIONS OR EXPRESS THOUGHTS IN A CLEAR AND CONVINCING WAY.

EVEN AN ARTICHOKE AND A SLIPPER MIGHT BECOME THE MAIN CHARACTERS IN A STORY. THE IMPORTANT THING IS TO CREATE CHARACTERS THAT ARE ORIGINAL, EITHER THROUGH YOUR WRITING OR BY STARTING WITH A DRAWING.

Human beings

Monsters, aliens, robots, supernatural creatures

Animals

Try this—draw a blank face and add various kinds of distinguishing features.

Hair

Mouth

Eyes

Nose

Once the elements are combined, your character will start to take shape.

Add clothes to the bodies to make them presentable.

But to create a character, it's not enough to give them a face, a body, and some clothes. All these elements must be fused with personality, to construct real characters that are ready to interpret the roles required by the plot. Try a variety of things and compare the results, until you find the most suitable solution.

Just like an actor, the same face changes according to the role.

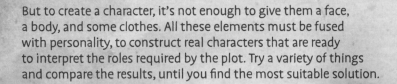

I NEED A DETECTIVE, A REAL TOUGH GUY!

Sometimes you have to make the unbelievable believable and vice versa. What you see is a police inspector from the 1930s who is tough and cynical but with a romantic side.

YOU HAVE TO ADMIT THAT EVERY NOW AND AGAIN YOU REALLY CAN JUDGE A BOOK BY ITS COVER!

Unlike a film, which benefits from the actor's voice, a graphic novel depends entirely on the character being immediately recognizable. It's a balancing act between distinctive elements.

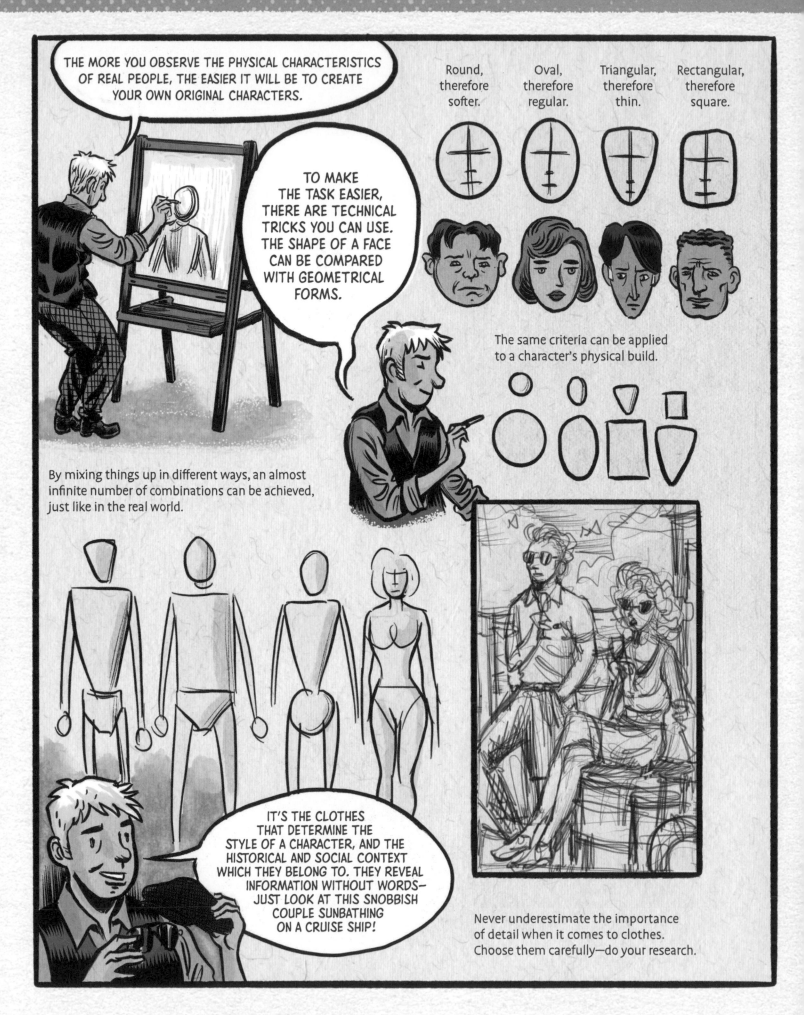

THE MORE YOU OBSERVE THE PHYSICAL CHARACTERISTICS OF REAL PEOPLE, THE EASIER IT WILL BE TO CREATE YOUR OWN ORIGINAL CHARACTERS.

TO MAKE THE TASK EASIER, THERE ARE TECHNICAL TRICKS YOU CAN USE. THE SHAPE OF A FACE CAN BE COMPARED WITH GEOMETRICAL FORMS.

Round, therefore softer.

Oval, therefore regular.

Triangular, therefore thin.

Rectangular, therefore square.

The same criteria can be applied to a character's physical build.

By mixing things up in different ways, an almost infinite number of combinations can be achieved, just like in the real world.

IT'S THE CLOTHES THAT DETERMINE THE STYLE OF A CHARACTER, AND THE HISTORICAL AND SOCIAL CONTEXT WHICH THEY BELONG TO. THEY REVEAL INFORMATION WITHOUT WORDS— JUST LOOK AT THIS SNOBBISH COUPLE SUNBATHING ON A CRUISE SHIP!

Never underestimate the importance of detail when it comes to clothes. Choose them carefully—do your research.

THE ROLE OF THE SETTING IS SO IMPORTANT, IT CAN TAKE ON THE SAME NARRATIVE WEIGHT AS A STORY'S CHARACTERS. HOW MANY TIMES HAS A STORY BEEN SUCCESSFUL BECAUSE OF THE PLACE IN WHICH IT WAS SET?

COUNTLESS TIMES!

Just think how much the same story can change depending on its setting:

A corridor in the office of a multinational corporation

The drawing room of a Victorian house

A forest of centuries-old oaks

YOU NEED TO DO SOME RESEARCH—LOOK FOR IMAGES IN BOOKS, CATALOGS, AND ONLINE.

IF YOU CAN, GO OUTSIDE AND WALK AROUND. LOOK FOR DETAILS TO INCLUDE.

TAKE PHOTOS, THINKING AS YOU GO ABOUT HOW THEY MIGHT BE USEFUL TO YOUR DRAWINGS.

CLICK

CLICK

It's best to use a 50 mm or 55 mm lens, which frames a view similar to the human eye and avoids the distorting effects of a wide-angle lens.

Don't forget the invaluable practice of drawing from life. Observe what surrounds you and reproduce it on paper—you can't beat it!

With a few tweaks, the same background can travel through time, creating wildly different settings.

The Middle Ages

The present day

A dystopian future

Obviously, a setting can also be drawn totally from your imagination. You may be inspired by places you know, remote places, or even ones you've dreamed up. The important thing is that they are relevant to the narrative.

MAKE SURE YOU TAKE THE GREATEST CARE WITH INTERIOR DÉCOR. AN AUTHOR MUST ALSO BE A DESIGNER!

Representations of the real world are generally drawn in perspective. Start by establishing your points of reference, which are:

the vanishing point, where the lines of perspective converge

the horizon line, where the viewer's gaze converges.

If you are basing your scenery on existing photographs or visual references, you might want to consider tracing them in pencil onto your work sheet.

60-degree set square

45-degree set square

DEFINE THE DETAILS AND INSERT THE ELEMENTS THAT GIVE YOUR NARRATIVE ITS PARTICULAR FEEL, FROM THE OBJECTS TO THE CHARACTERS.

AND THERE YOU HAVE YOUR SETTING, READY TO BE INKED!

Use a ruler and set squares to obtain a sharper, more precise line. The choice depends on your style of drawing and the story. Differentiate the figures in the foreground from those in the background by modifying your marks. Or else let your characters and the setting fuse into a single environment.

YOU CAN INK YOUR SCENERY WITH ANY NUMBER OF TOOLS. MANY ARTISTS USE FINELINERS (OR MULTI-LINERS), VARYING THE THICKNESS OF THE NIB. IF YOU INK FREEHAND, YOUR MARKS WILL HAVE MORE LIFE.

The important thing, as always, is not to lose sight of the story. The story always comes first!

YOU NEED A STORYBOARD IN ORDER TO TAKE YOUR STORY FROM SCRIPT TO LAYOUT.

IF YOU'RE THE CREATOR OF BOTH THE WORDS AND THE PICTURES, YOU COULD THEORETICALLY SKIP THE PROCESS OF WRITING A SCRIPT AND GO STRAIGHT TO STORYBOARDING.

THE STORYBOARD IS YOUR BLUEPRINT AND YOUR WORKSHOP. IT'S LIKE A COMPOSER'S SCORE, A SCIENTIST'S LABORATORY, AN ALCHEMIST'S CAVE.

It's within the storyboard that ideas introduced in the storyline and developed in the script take on a definite narrative rhythm. This rhythm will determine the way you tell your story.

TAKE A PENCIL AND ERASER AND BEGIN. FEEL FREE TO CHANGE YOUR MIND AS OFTEN AS YOU LIKE.

IMMERSE YOURSELF IN THE STORY AND TRANSFER IT ONTO PAPER, ONE PAGE AFTER ANOTHER.

The pages you draw are like the cars of a train running along a temporary track. They will allow you to establish the rhythm of the narrative, correcting the script if you need to, changing the sequence of events, introducing flashbacks, and flashforwards.

WRITE A DRAFT VERSION OF THE DIALOGUE AND THE CAPTIONS IN THE BALLOONS. DO THIS IN PENCIL – YOU'RE BOUND TO WANT TO MAKE CHANGES LATER.

FOR A BETTER OVERALL VIEW, YOU CAN HANG YOUR STORYBOARD ON THE WALL.

OR EVEN LAY IT ON THE FLOOR.

The drawings might be barely sketched or so well defined that they can act as your final penciled pages.

The size can vary, too. You might choose to draw the storyboard at the same size as the final version, or in a smaller format so you can put the pages side by side in sequence and establish the story's rhythm.

AND NOW YOU CAN GET DOWN TO SOME SERIOUS DRAWING!

MAKE YOURSELF COMFORTABLE AND ARRANGE ALL YOUR EQUIPMENT ON THE DESK IN FRONT OF YOU.

It's very important to have a workstation that's roomy and comfortable. A good ergonomic chair is best for your back, and you should also have a good lamp with a cool white bulb, to protect your eyes from strain.

Always keep an outline of the narrative and your storyboard close at hand. They are the road you will follow.

Start with your penciled layouts (either analog or digital). Work through these again and again, until the details are right. The next stage is inking, and here you can let it rip, using anything from a fountain pen to a ballpoint. The great graphic novelist Alberto Breccia actually used razor blades!

COLORS TELL THE STORY!

DAB SMALL WASHES OF YOUR CHOSEN COLORS ON A SHEET OF PAPER, ARRANGING THEM SIDE BY SIDE, ACCORDING TO THEIR INTENSITY. YOU CAN ARRANGE THEM BY SCENE, SETTING OR SITUATION.

THE COMBINATIONS ARE INFINITE:

Next, move on to the coloring. We've already talked about coloring techniques, so let's concentrate here on choosing the right color palette. The juxtaposition of colors is fundamental to a graphic novel's overall aesthetic and to the atmosphere of each drawing.

TONAL

HARMONIC

CONTRASTING

COMPLEMENTARY

RAINBOW

MONOCHROMATIC

After the coloring, the digital post-production and the lettering, we're almost done! Now comes the editing stage and the printing. Just be patient and you'll soon have your beautiful graphic novel in your hands, and take it from me, that's always an exciting moment!

YOU'VE FINISHED DRAWING, NOW WHAT?

You have your script, you've drawn all the panels, but obviously that's not all. The **FINAL STAGE IS TO PUT EVERYTHING TOGETHER IN LAYOUT AND TO CREATE YOUR BOOK**. Page layouts, lettering, and correcting the proofs are essential stages in the process of creating a graphic novel. And if you've come this far, why not think about pitching it to a publisher, and going to a comics fair to meet fellow graphic novelists?!

PAGE LAYOUT

Do you remember on page 20 when you set up your script document with page numbers? This is the stage where accurate pagination counts for something. To create a page layout start by importing the illustrations into a graphics program like Adobe InDesign.

Import them in sequence, but remember that your file starts with the **first page** of the book—the **title page**. The title page is a single right-hand page and usually includes the book's title.

SPACE ODDITY

The **last page** of the book is a single left-hand page and might include legal information—in which case it would be referred to as **the copyright page**.

GRAB A BOOK AND CHECK FOR YOURSELF

When you calculate the total number of the pages needed for your book (see page 25), you will need to add at least these two pages to your total.

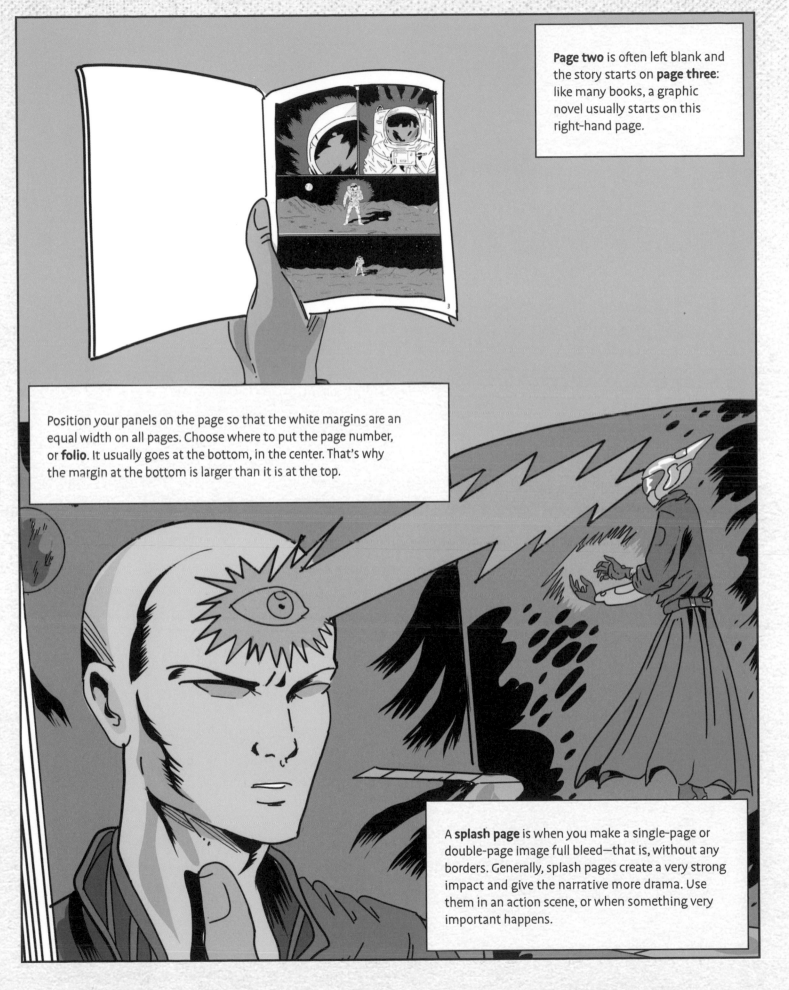

Page two is often left blank and the story starts on page three: like many books, a graphic novel usually starts on this right-hand page.

Position your panels on the page so that the white margins are an equal width on all pages. Choose where to put the page number, or **folio**. It usually goes at the bottom, in the center. That's why the margin at the bottom is larger than it is at the top.

A **splash page** is when you make a single-page or double-page image full bleed—that is, without any borders. Generally, splash pages create a very strong impact and give the narrative more drama. Use them in an action scene, or when something very important happens.

In comics, **lettering** refers to both the positioning and drawing of the balloons and captions, and the positioning of the words themselves inside the balloons and captions, in a style of hand-drawn font that is characteristic of comics.

Lettering is also the thought bubbles and the drawings of sound effects and noises, in all their various forms and graphic styles.

It's standard to typeset all text as far as possible (using either a preexisting font or one created by you) rather than lettering the full text by hand, because it makes any later corrections and changes to the text that much easier.

Remember this basic rule: the text should aim to fill the shape of the balloon.

PROOFREADING

Typesetting the text inside the balloons and the captions is a delicate operation, which requires a lot of care. Even really experienced people can sometimes make mistakes when importing the text from the script into the page layout. The script itself may have some typos. So after you've inserted all the text, it's important to reread every page carefully, looking for mistakes.

PLEASE WILL YOU REREAD IT FOR ME?

OK, BUT IN RETURN YOU HAVE TO COME FISHING WITH ME THIS WEEKEND! HAHAHAHA!

I also recommend asking someone with fresh eyes to read your graphic novel. Someone who hasn't read it before is more likely to see all the mistakes you've missed.

This is a specialist task, which in publishing houses is entrusted to experienced desk editors.

DAMN! WE ONLY HAVE THREE HOURS TO CORRECT ALL THESE PAGES!

DEADLINES

Every piece of work you do, from the simplest task to the most creative development work, needs a cut-off point. If you start your graphic novel without a fixed deadline, you might never finish it.

There will always be something more urgent to distract you. A professional graphic novel artist, for example, can easily draw a page per day on average, from the storyboard to the coloring.

Obviously, if you start by creating a storyboard for the entire book first before moving on to the penciling, inking, and coloring, this average of a page per day may only apply at the end of the process.

But it's still a useful indication for giving your work a time limit.

GETTING PUBLISHED

Even if you set out to make your graphic novel purely for your own enjoyment, you still might want to think about pitching it to a publisher.

IN MY OPINION YOU SHOULD GET IT PUBLISHED! IT'S BEAUTIFUL!

First of all, look for stories that are similar to yours and find out who the publisher is. Discover new publishers by looking at books in ...

... bookstores ...

... libraries ...

... and online.

EDIT N 5
BD

If you think your graphic novel would fit well alongside a publishing house's other titles, then send it to them. But don't stop with two or three publishers: the more publishers you send your book to, the more chances there are it will succeed.

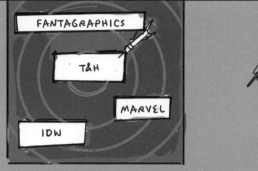

Most publishing houses have a general e-mail address on their website for sending proposals to, and advice on what format to send it in.

WILL THEY EVER ANSWER ME?!?

You may think it's a waste of time, but it isn't. You never know when the graphic novel you've created could be what an editor or agent is looking for.

It's never easy, obviously, but it is always worth a try. Especially if you present your work well and your graphic novel grabs their attention!

HEY, LOOK WHAT I JUST GOT!

Alternatively, your work might be pitched to publishers by an agent, but finding a good agent is harder than finding a taxi in New York... and almost harder than finding a good publisher!

INTERNATIONAL COMIC BOOK FAIRS

Discovering the world of graphic novels can of course happen in bookstores, comic book stores, and online, but nothing compares to the feeling you get when you go to a comic book fair.

The world of graphic novels in one place. All your favorite authors and publishers, one after the other. A program of events, presentations, and signings you wouldn't even dream of finding in Wonderland.

Fairs are a great opportunity to discover new books, to get your favorites signed, and to find new editions and collectors' items. But above all, it's only at fairs that you can really see what works and what doesn't. It's here that you can deepen your knowledge, your feel and your taste for graphic novels. And maybe meet the right person to send your work to!

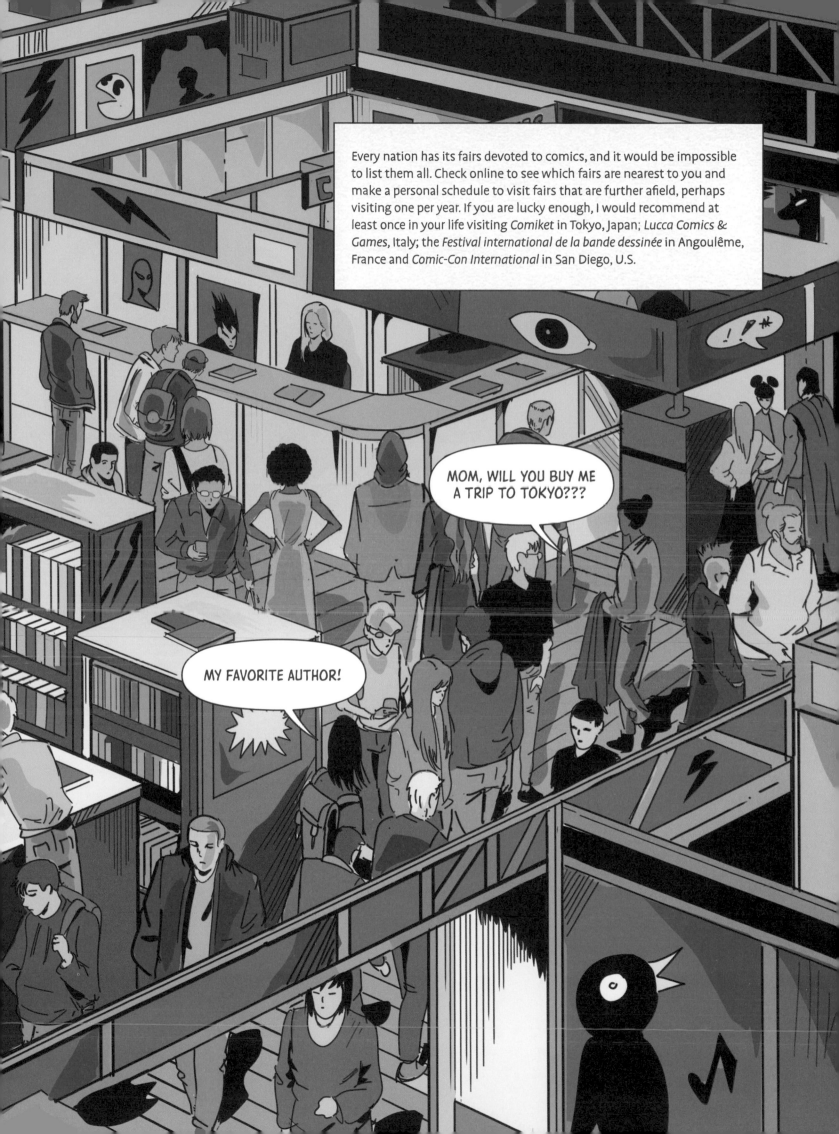

CULT CREATORS

The authors I'd like to introduce to you here are **PART OF THE PANTHEON OF COMIC BOOKS AND GRAPHIC NOVELS**. Obviously there are many more but these are the ones I think **EVERYONE SHOULD KNOW ABOUT**. You can find the books I mention on page 96 under Reading List.

JACKIE ORMES
U.S. 1911-1985

At a time when the comics industry was dominated by men, Jackie Ormes blazed her own trail. Her first comic strip about the adventures of Torchy Brown, a teenager who moves from Mississippi to New York, was published in the *Pittsburgh Courier* in 1937.

Ormes represented African American women as fashionable, independent, and socially engaged, defying the stereotypes of the time. She was the first African American woman to have a comic strip published in a weekly, nationally distributed newspaper. Through her characters, she discussed and confronted racism, environmental concerns, and other social and political topics. Ormes was truly ahead of her time.

Considered a master by the generations of comic book authors who came after him, Eisner had the honor, while he was still alive, of seeing a prize named after him—the Eisner Award.

WILL EISNER
U.S. 1917-2005

In 1940 he started publishing stories about The Spirit, a masked detective and criminologist with a mysterious past.

He was among the first creatives in the industry to use the term "graphic novel," for his 1978 book *A Contract with God*.

ALBERTO BRECCIA
ARGENTINA, 1919-1993

Born in Uruguay, Breccia moved to Argentina at the age of three. He established a high benchmark for graphic novelists the world over because of his ability to experiment stylistically and the difficult themes he tackled in his work.

He was the illustrator of Juan Sasturain's *Perramus*, a graphic novel about a political dissident, which was awarded an Amnesty International Prize in 1989. His original use of India ink and his constant pictorial experimentation make him a master worth studying, even now.

A comic book artist and writer with an adventurous life, Hugo Pratt created one of the most iconic graphic novel characters, Corto Maltese, who appeared for the first time in *The Ballad of the Salty Sea*. Published at the end of the 1960s, this book is considered one of the first graphic novels. Corto Maltese is a mysterious hero, a sailor, and a non-conformist.

In Pratt's works, the historical and geographical reconstructions are true to life and the characters' psychologies are explored in great depth.

OSAMU TEZUKA
JAPAN, 1928–1989

They called him the father, or God, of manga, and there's no doubt that without him manga would be very different. Tezuka has been credited with establishing the style of large eyes on manga characters, borrowed from American comic book artists like Max Fleischer and Walt Disney.

He made his debut in the mid-1940s and introduced what remains his most famous character, Astro Boy, in 1951. Tezuka also made an anime adaptation of *Astro Boy*, becoming a pioneer in this field, too. There are many legends and anecdotes about him, such as his love for the natural world and insects. Tezuka's assistant, Toshio Ban, serialized Tezuka's life story in a manga-style biography, *The Osamu Tezuka Story: A Life in Manga and Anime*, which is essential reading.

Although he is best known for his work in fantasy and science fiction, few can compare with Moebius for the level of experimentation and variety he brought to the field of graphic novels. He produced drawings for texts by Alejandro Jodorowsky, wrote a manga with Jirō Taniguchi, and collaborated on science fiction films such as *Tron* and *Alien*. Rightly considered one of the greatest and most prolific graphic novel masters, he wrote and drew an incredible number of works.

RIYOKO IKEDA
JAPAN, B. 1947

The Rose of Versailles, also known as *Lady Oscar*, by Riyoko Ikeda, is a must-read manga for lovers of comics and anime. A highly original artist, Ikeda is also famous for *The Window of Orpheus*, a work that cemented historical settings and androgynous women as her favorite subjects.

In 2008, the French government awarded her the Légion d'Honneur for helping to spread French culture, making her the first mangaka (or manga artist) to receive this honor. Also in the 2000s, at the age of almost 50, she launched a separate career as an opera singer.

ART SPIEGELMAN
SWEDEN / USA, B.1948

Before telling you about Art Spiegelman, I recommend that you read his most famous work, *MAUS*. Once you have read it, come back here . You will realize there is very little for me to add that you won't already have discovered by reading *MAUS*. (Just to be clear, I don't think it's right to force anyone to do anything, but if I were ever to discover that *MAUS* had been made compulsory reading for everyone, I would be happy!)

RAW

Art Spiegelman was born in Stockholm and moved to the United States when he was young, along with his parents, two Polish Jews who had survived Auschwitz. He was a part of the underground "comix" movement in San Francisco in the 1970s, and since then has edited comics and taught graphic arts as well as making his own work. *MAUS*, his most famous work, tells the story of his father during the Holocaust.

ALAN MOORE
UK, B. 1953

Few graphic novelists have achieved such consistency between who they are and what they do as Alan Moore. He started his career as an illustrator before devoting himself entirely to writing. He worked as an author and screenwriter, and produced a large output of work, but most readers will know him for his comic-books-turned-blockbuster-films, *V for Vendetta* and *Watchmen*.

As a child, he was a big fan of superhero comic books by Marvel and DC Comics, publishers he later worked for. He brought an introspective, psychological dimension of great literary worth to the superhero genre.

A visionary author and screenwriter, Gaiman first came to fame in the 1980s with *The Sandman*, a saga that fundamentally influenced the development of the contemporary graphic novel.

Around the same time, DC comics were looking for writers who could help bring the universe of superheroes to an adult audience, and hired Gaiman to write comics, including *Black Orchid*.

In his work, Gaiman combines mythology, history, philosophy, and psychology to create literary graphic novels that are completely unique in the publishing world.

MARJANE SATRAPI
IRAN / FRANCE, B.1969

There are moments when an author realizes that they have written a good book, which—with time—may even become a classic. But imagine a scenario when your own life story strikes you as so crazy and symbolic that it urgently needs to be written, and becomes essential reading for an entire generation of young people.

Persepolis, Marjane Satrapi's most famous work, was born out of her own life story. Satrapi realized that the story she, her family, and her country of Iran had lived through, during and after the Iranian Revolution, needed to be told. In her other graphic novels, including *Chicken with Plums* and *Embroideries*, she has continued to tell stories about life in Iran, blending the personal and the historical. I don't know when Satrapi realized how significant her story was, but it's a question you should ask yourself every now and again—could what you're living through be worth writing about, if not for your benefit, then for other people's?

JILLIAN TAMAKI
CANADA, B. 1980

Its events are private and intimate, and yet universally relatable, touching on subjects that cross the borders of time or place.

Tamaki turned her hand to web comics in *SuperMutant Magic Academy*, as well as graphic short stories in *Boundless*. Although her work dwells on apparently simple things, insignificant details, and memories that fade, they all conceal great truth. Much like the story you're thinking of writing, isn't that so?

Jillian Tamaki began making comics in 2003. Her award-winning graphic novel *This One Summer*, drawn by Jillian Tamaki and written by her cousin Mariko Tamaki, is both famous and infamous—listed among the American Library Association's most challenging books, for its explorations of sexuality and drug use. It is as light as a summer memory of that time in our lives when we move from childhood to adolescence, but it leaves an impression on those who read it that's as deep as the ocean.

CREATOR INTERVIEWS

It's time to hear from some experienced **GRAPHIC NOVELISTS IN THEIR OWN WORDS.** The following interviews provide an insight into the creative practices of five authors. Their diversity of process, style, and sources of inspiration are proof that **THERE IS NO ONE WAY TO DRAW A GRAPHIC NOVEL!**

NINA BUNJEVAC

IS A SERBIAN-CANADIAN GRAPHIC NOVELIST
BORN IN 1973 IN WELLAND, CANADA

When did you start drawing?

I began drawing at a very young age. In fact, it was so early that I do not recall exactly when. It seems like it's always been a part of my life.

Who were your teachers?

My grandmother and my grandfather. He taught me how to hold a pencil, she instilled a love of learning in me.

Do you have three tips for young artists?

1. Don't skip the steps in art education.
2. Refrain from following the trends in art.
3. Learn something new every day.

Where does the creative process start for you: on paper, in the mind or in both "places" at the same time? And where do you mainly draw your inspiration from?

The creative process takes place equally on paper as it does in the mind. The idea part, naturally, starts in the mind. It often feels as if the ideas come out of nowhere, and they tend to come when I least expect them. As far as the inspiration goes, it comes from areas of interest I am passionate about: independent and noir cinema, depth psychology, history, mythology, and alchemy. It's very important for an artist to keep growing and learning.

ᐯ❯ Below: sketches from *La Réparation*

< Left: sketches from *La Réparation*

Do you prefer to work in an analog way or digitally? Why?

I do analog about 85%, and digital about 15%. I sketch exclusively by hand, but then I scan my sketches and manipulate them in Photoshop. That is, I will clean them, resize, and reposition them. The final sketch is then printed out, and transferred onto good paper over the light table. All inking is done by hand. Final drawings are scanned and cleaned up in Photoshop. This seems to work for me quite well, as it saves time, especially when having to resize an element, and it saves on the amount of paper used.

Are there stories that you think can be better told in comics than with another artistic language? If so, why are graphic novels better?

Graphic novels work very well in education,

especially when tackling the themes of history, mythology, or social issues. Comics are a great way of making education and learning fun.

What do you love most about graphic novels?

Versatility in terms of genre and style. There is so much room for experimentation.

What do you love most about your job?

Free travel when it comes to book tours and festivals; flexible hours as well.

How many unpublished stories do you still have in the "drawer"?

I do not have any unpublished stories, but I do have three stories that were never finished.

ELISA MACELLARI

IS A THAI-ITALIAN GRAPHIC NOVELIST, BORN IN 1981 IN PERUGIA, ITALY

When did you start to draw?

I started when I was little, as soon as I learned to hold a pencil in my hand. Drawing was always my favorite activity. I copied what I had around me, my room, my games, the drawings in books. Later, I enrolled at the Academy of Fine Arts and it took up most of my time.

What do you like to draw?

I love drawing jungles, plants, and floral patterns, mysterious creatures, strange objects, and wild animals. I love apes, especially gibbons. Their anatomy is really fascinating.

Do you have three pieces of advice for young artists?

Draw a lot and don't be afraid. Sometimes, the most effective things are what we do instinctively. Try to understand who we really are and where we come from, always be honest in your drawing, and avoid imitating other people. Keep trying and never get discouraged if you make mistakes. Mistakes are essential if you want to do good work.

Where does the creative process start for you: on the paper, in your head, or in both "places" at the same time? And where do you mainly draw your inspiration from?

My main inspiration is travel. I rarely draw on the spot, but I take home with me a large number of photographs, stories, faces, decorations, and details that have struck me. Then there's a period when I process it all mentally and what I've discovered comes out at all sorts of different times. The most surprising connections are the unexpected ones.

∨ Below: Pages from *Kusama: The Graphic Novel*

∧ Above: Sketches from *Papaya Salad*

Do you prefer to work in analog or in digital? Why?

As far as I'm concerned, technique should match the idea we have in our minds. So sometimes it works better to draw in analog, sometimes in digital.

Are there stories you think it's easier to talk about in comic books than in any other artistic form? And if so, why?

I like human stories; stories about people, things they have really experienced and that we can empathize and identify with. Comics make it possible to talk about external landscapes but also about inner worlds, which aren't easy to visualize in any other way. Comics allow us to move easily between inner and outer worlds, and also to make people listen really attentively.

What do you like most about your work?

The ability to express the thoughts that I wouldn't be able to bring out just with words, and the chance to touch the lives of people I don't know, even in a small way, through a book or an illustration.

BEN PASSMORE

IS AN AMERICAN GRAPHIC NOVELIST BORN IN 1983 IN MASSACHUSETTS, U.S.

When did you start drawing?

I probably started drawing when I was very little, like most people do. At a certain point I knew it was a passion for me because I would get these expensive magazines about the superhero comics and spend all day trying to draw Batman like Jim Lee. Never quite pulled off a Jim Lee-like style though.

What do you love to draw?

I don't know if I love drawing, it's more of an extension of myself. Maybe I love it in the same way I love awkward parts of my body. A lot of young boys are taught to suppress things that

don't show off how tough you are, and drawing was this reassuring light I kept in a dark hidden place, that reminded me of who I was. It was a strange transition to make it my job, but then again, I feel seen on the page more than in real life most of the time.

Do you have three tips for young artists?

Being young now is a lot different than it was for me. Your life was a lot more private as a default and you had to work pretty hard to get your work in front of your friends, never mind total strangers. So I would always keep a part of yourself for yourself, go out and have interesting experiences that are

< Left:
Daygloayhole,
Issue Three

∧ Above: artwork from *City Of Brotherly Riots*
< Left: artwork from *Sports Is Hell*

only for you. Make special time to draw things you don't like to draw, when you're drowning in complicated work and deadlines it'll help you in ways you won't expect.

Where does the creative process start for you: on paper, in the mind, or in both "places" at the same time? And where do you mainly draw your inspiration from?

Despite a lot of my work tackling socio-political issues, I usually start each comic with questioning where my personal investment in the topic is. I'll take a walk around my block and then sit down and write notes and phrases that come to mind. Sometimes I won't know the answer to the question until I've done a lot of research and taken a few more walks.

How might a young graphic novel fan persuade an adult who doesn't like graphic novels to read them?

Honestly I feel like it's more often the other way around in the US; older people trying to persuade young people into enjoying comics. For me the ritual of going to the bookstore and finding

something is beautiful. This kind of treasure hunt is a strong cultural element of loving comics that I try and share with people.

What do you love most about graphic novels?

The comics I like the most are almost always an individual's singular vision. Someone who was so weighted down with an idea that they closed themselves up in a room and came out with this book. Reading it always feels like you've been given the key to someone's brain. It's really exciting. I don't think any other kind of art feels that way to me.

Is there a story you would like to make now? Can you tell me about it?

The first thing I want to do after I complete a project is to make a sequel to it. It always feels like there's more I want to say about a topic, or more I want to do with the characters. I don't know if that's enthusiasm or bad writing. I used to do a dystopian sci-fi series before having a career in non-fiction, I always think about getting back to that.

PETER KUPER

IS AN AMERICAN GRAPHIC NOVELIST
BORN IN 1958 IN NEW JERSEY, U.S.

When did you start drawing?

Like most kids, I scribbled as soon as I could hold a crayon. A few times I did a drawing that seemed like something good, but really I didn't start more seriously until I was about fifteen and began keeping a sketchbook.

Who were your teachers?

Throughout the years I had several. I went to art school, but looking at art in museums and reading comics and other books were the best teachers.

What do you love to draw?

Insects—my other love and interest. All kinds.

Do you have three tips for young artists?

1) Failure comes with the process, if you can pick yourself up afterward and continue again the next day with enthusiasm, you can have a shot at a career. Everybody fails at some point and sometimes regularly!
2) Do something you love, so figure out what you're passionate about. You are only promised an audience of one (yourself) so if you do work you think someone else will like and they don't, you could end up with no audience.
3) Don't worry about having a style. Styles are like clothes—if you wear them too long, they start to smell.
4) Bonus tip! Even if it doesn't become a career, don't stop drawing, just the act of putting pen to paper can be a joy and worring about using it to make a living can sometimes rob that joy.

Is there a rituality in your work?

Drawing is like exercising—if you do it regularly you will crave it. If you don't, you get out of practice and do less and less. If I don't draw regularly, I become sad. So, I'm motivated to draw. It can be a form of therapy.

Do you prefer to work in an analog way or digitally? Why?

I do both but always try to start on paper. I like the direct connection I get with pen, pencil, or brush in hand. Also, I sell my original art. This is a good part of my income and with digital you can only sell prints, which is less valuable, and less interesting to look at.

Is there a place in the world, or a historical era, that in your opinion can be best described through the medium of the graphic novel?

There are topics like, say, the Holocaust, that are hard to comprehend, but a book, like Art Spiegelman's *Maus*, demonstrated comics could make this difficult subject accessible to a wide audience. Anthropomorphizing the characters—Jews as mice, Nazis as cats—made the story universal.

Are there stories that you think can be better told in comics than with another artistic language? If so, why are graphic novels better?

It's an art form that simultaneously lets characters say things, think things, and play with visuals that

∧ Above: Line art from *INterSECTS*

∧ Above: Sketch from *Heart Of Darkness*

can be ironic and in contrast to the text and use words as visual elements—all in one panel!

What do you love most about graphic novels?

They can be as powerful as a movie or a play or a book or a painting, all rolled into one form. They can be simply drawn with complicated text or vice versa. That's the very short answer! Comics have a unique, intimate relationship to readers. They ask the reader to connect dots on every page and engage and interpret. Reading comics is not a passive experience.

What do you love most about your job?

It doesn't feel like a job and I generally work seven days a week.

How many unpublished stories do you still have in the "drawer"?

Several original graphic novels fully developed (though not completely drawn) at least two adaptations that were started (Camus's *The Plague* and William Golding's *Lord of The Flies*). Like I said, failure is common.

Is there a story you would like to make now? Can you tell me about it?

I am in my third year working on a graphic novel called *INterSECTS*. It is a history of insects and the people who have studied them. I have another year to go to complete it while juggling my other work, but this is the project I have been wanting to find my whole life.

KAN TAKAHAMA

IS A JAPANESE MANGAKA
BORN IN 1977 IN AMAKUSA, JAPAN

Who were your teachers?

I was taught to draw as a child by my parents. They were both art teachers. At junior high school, I belonged to an art club, where I learned about design from the art teachers, and then I went to a senior high school that had an art program. So I've been exposed to drawing throughout my entire life, but I've never actually been taught how to draw manga. Since I didn't know how to draw manga at first, I just started drawing in my own style.

What do you love to draw?

When I started out, I loved drawing elderly people. At that time, there were lots of stories about young people, so I wanted to do something different, and I liked drawing elderly people's bodies and movements. Recently, I've been drawing a lot of stories set in the past. I prefer historical stories to contemporary dramas.

Do you have three tips for young artists?

Three things that experience has taught me about drawing manga are:
1. Before starting to draw, it is important to get all your information together. This will get rid of inconsistencies in the story and remove the need to change it later to make it make sense.
2. If you decide to become a manga artist, I recommend being aware from the start that you will remain a manga artist until you retire. That way, it will naturally become clear to you what you should draw. Even if you feel impatient when you see your contemporaries publishing bestsellers, you'll keep learning what to do and you won't be led astray.
3. Write down your strengths and weaknesses. Do you have strengths that you want to develop further or skills that are lacking? Taking stock of yourself once a year, such as during the Christmas break, and clarifying the skills you want to acquire or the things you want to do is a good refresher.

Where does the creative process start for you: on paper, in the mind or in both "places" at the same time? And where do you mainly draw your inspiration from?

Gathering the material comes first. Once I have decided on a theme, before creating the story or the characters, I collect information. I make a notebook, and I draw what I have researched. That way, by the time I've finished gathering the material, the characters and the story almost

create themselves. This was the method used by scriptwriters in the golden age of Japanese films. I recommend that everyone tries it. It's very effective, especially when you're drawing historical stories or a particular area of expertise, such as that of an artisan. Perhaps it can also be applied to romance manga.

Do you prefer to work in an analog way or digitally? Why?

I like both, and I've tried both, but in the end, I can't decide. I go back and forth between the two. But tablets are always evolving, so I might go digital in the future. I think that working in an analog way is less tiring on the eyes, back, and shoulders, though.

How might a young graphic novel fan persuade an adult who doesn't like graphic novels to read them?

Maybe there's no need to persuade adults. People read what they like. In Japan, the tide has changed completely in the past few decades, with adults coming to appreciate manga. Parents, relatives, teachers, they all read my manga now. I think that as an author grows up, matures, and their interests change, their readers are also drawn from corresponding age groups.

Young manga artists should draw what they like without worrying about whether adults will be bored by it. If today's younger generation creates good work, the tide is sure to change in other countries too someday.

Are there stories that you think can be better told in comics than with another artistic language? If so, why are graphic novels better?

I haven't really thought about that either. But the budget of a graphic novel is nothing, compared to a movie, so it's possible to create something gorgeous on a low budget. Although, of course a lot of research needs to be done.

What do you love most about graphic novels?

I love the fact that, unlike in movies, the characters do exactly what you want without the need to make unreasonable demands on actors. Compared to novels, the good thing is that you can see the characters.

Images from the Book *Invincibles*, Massot Editions 2021
< Left: Character design
> Right: Script
> Right: Finished page

INDEX

READING LIST

Toshio Ban, *The Osamu Tezuka Story: A Life in Manga and Anime*
Alberto Breccia and Juan Sasturain, *Perramus*
Will Eisner, *A Contract with God*
Neil Gaiman, *The Sandman*
Riyoko Ikeda, *The Rose of Versailles*
Moebius and Alejandro Jodorowsky, *The Incal*
Scott McCloud, *Understanding Comics*
Alan Moore and David Lloyd, *V for Vendetta*
Hugo Pratt, *The Ballad of the Salty Sea*
Marjanne Satrapi, *Persepolis*
Art Spiegelman, *Maus*
Jillian and Mariko Tamaki, *This One Summer*
Osamu Tezuka, *Astro Boy*